W9-CDD-630

STONES
OF REMEMBRANCE

BIBLE STUDY GUIDE

From the Bible-teaching ministry of

Charles R. Swindoll

INSIGHT FOR LIVING

Chuck graduated in 1963 from Dallas Theological Seminary, where he now serves as the school's fourth president, helping to prepare a new generation of men and women for the ministry. Chuck has served in pastorates in three states: Massachusetts, Texas, and California, including almost twenty-three years at the First Evangelical Free Church in Fullerton, California. His sermon messages have been aired over radio since 1979 as the *Insight for Living* broadcast. A best-selling author, Chuck has written numerous books and booklets on many subjects.

Based on the outlines and transcripts of Chuck's sermons, the study guide text is co-authored by Ken Gire, a graduate of Texas Christian University and Dallas Theological Seminary. The Living Insights are written by Gary Matlack, a graduate of Texas Tech University and Dallas Theological Seminary.

Editor in Chief:
Cynthia Swindoll

Coauthor of Text:
Ken Gire

Author of Living Insights:
Gary Matlack

Assistant Editor:
Wendy Peterson

Copy Editor:
Tom Kimber

Text Designer:
Gary Lett

Publishing System Specialist:
Bob Haskins

Director, Communications and Marketing Division:
Deedee Snyder

Marketing Manager:
Alene Cooper

Project Coordinator:
Colette Muse

Production Manager:
John Norton

Printer:
Sinclair Printing Company

Unless otherwise identified, all Scripture references are from the New American Standard Bible, © The Lockman Foundation 1960, 1962, 1963, 1968, 1971, 1972, 1973, 1975, 1977. Used by permission. The other translation cited is the King James Version [KJV].

An effort has been made to locate sources and obtain permission where necessary for the quotations used in this book. In the event of any unintentional omission, a modification will gladly be incorporated in future printings.

ISBN 0-8499-8402-5
COVER DESIGN: Nina Paris
COVER PHOTOGRAPH: Rudi Weislein
Printed in the United States of America

CONTENTS

INTRODUCTION

What a strange memorial!

A stack of twelve large stones stood in a heap. They had been taken from the Jordan when Joshua and the Hebrews had crossed over the riverbed en route to Canaan. God had dried up the river so His people could cross over, as He had done at the Red Sea forty years earlier. Therefore, Joshua was instructed to leave the stack of stones as a remembrance for generations to come. When children yet to be born would ask their parents, "What do these stones mean?" they would be told of God's mighty acts and be encouraged to reverence Him forever. The account is recorded in Joshua 4.

This miniseries includes four strong statements about the greatness of our God. They stand like a silent memorial, solid as stone, to remind all of us that the Lord God is still deserving of our highest honor. Like none other, He is sovereign, merciful, faithful, and holy.

As we acknowledge each attribute, may our respect for Him be glorified, may our fear of Him be intensified, and may our praise to Him be magnified.

Chuck Swindoll

PUTTING TRUTH
INTO ACTION

Knowledge apart from application falls short of God's desire for His children. He wants us to apply what we learn so that we will change and grow. This study guide was prepared with these goals in mind. As you go through the following pages, we hope your desire to discover biblical truth will grow as your understanding of God's Word increases and that you will be encouraged to apply what you've learned.

To assist you in your study, we've included a section called 🌺 **Living Insights** at the end of each lesson. These exercises will challenge you to study further and to think of specific ways to put your discoveries into action.

There are many ways to use this guide—in personal devotions, group studies, discussions with friends and family, and Sunday school classes. And, of course, it's an ideal study aid when you're listening to its corresponding *Insight for Living* radio series.

To benefit most from this study guide, we would encourage you to consider it a spiritual journal. That's why we've included space in the **Living Insights** for recording your thoughts and discoveries. We hope you'll return to those sections often for review and encouragement as you continue to grow in your walk with Christ.

Ken Gire

Ken Gire
Coauthor of Text

Gary Matlack

Gary Matlack
Author of Living Insights

STONES
OF REMEMBRANCE

Chapter 1

GOD'S SOVEREIGNTY

Daniel 4:24–37; Job 38, 42; Romans 11:33–36

At the height of his military career, Napoleon was asked if God was on the side of France. The world conqueror cynically replied, "God is on the side with the heaviest artillery."

Then came Waterloo.

Napoleon not only lost that battle but his empire as well. Years later, in exile on the island of St. Helena, the broken military genius humbly acknowledged, "Man proposes; God disposes."

Thus, in a painfully abrasive rub with reality, Napoleon came to believe in the sovereignty of God and the truth of Proverbs 21:31:

> The horse is prepared for the day of battle,
> But victory belongs to the Lord.

Who's in Charge around Here?

Few doctrines have caused a greater theological stir than the sovereignty of God. Within the vortex of that controversy swirls the question: "Who's in charge—God or man?" It seems a question everyone asks at some time in life. Today we'll look at two men who did: one from his perch on top of the world, the other from his sorrowful place at the bottom.

Nebuchadnezzar's Delusions

Most of Daniel 4 centers on a dialogue between the prophet Daniel and King Nebuchadnezzar. The king has had a disturbing dream and tries in vain to have it interpreted. The dream baffles his wise men and mystics, so Daniel is brought in. Not only does Daniel interpret the dream, but he talks straight to the prideful heart of the dreamer.

> "'This is the interpretation, O king, and this is the
> decree of the Most High, which has come upon my

1

lord the king: that you be driven away from mankind, and your dwelling place be with the beasts of the field, and you be given grass to eat like cattle and be drenched with the dew of heaven; and seven periods of time will pass over you, *until you recognize* that the Most High is ruler over the realm of mankind, and bestows it on whomever He wishes. And in that it was commanded to leave the stump with the roots of the tree, your kingdom will be assured to you *after you recognize* that it is Heaven that rules.'" (vv. 24–26, emphasis added)

"Until you recognize . . . after you recognize." The word *acknowledge* more precisely captures the powerful intent of the original than the translation *recognize*. Daniel is not urging the deluded king to merely observe but to radically accept and embrace the truth that "the Most High is ruler over the realm of mankind . . . that it is Heaven that rules." Twelve months later, Daniel's prophecy is fulfilled.

"The king reflected and said, 'Is this not Babylon the great, which I myself have built as a royal residence by the might of my power and for the glory of my majesty?' While the word was in the king's mouth, a voice came from heaven, saying, 'King Nebuchadnezzar, to you it is declared: sovereignty has been removed from you, and you will be driven away from mankind, and your dwelling place will be with the beasts of the field. You will be given grass to eat like cattle, and seven periods of time will pass over you, until you recognize that the Most High is ruler over the realm of mankind, and bestows it on whomever He wishes.'" (vv. 30–32)

God—not man—is in charge of the earth, and that includes Babylon. Nebuchadnezzar's sovereignty is only a delegated rule, not an absolute one. In time, the deposed and humbled king comes to realize this.

"But at the end of that period I, Nebuchadnezzar, raised my eyes toward heaven, and my reason returned to me, and I blessed the Most High and praised and honored Him who lives forever. . . . Now I Nebuchadnezzar praise, exalt, and honor the

King of heaven, for all His works are true and His ways just, and He is able to humble those who walk in pride." (vv. 34, 37)

When Nebuchadnezzar came to his senses, his delusions of grandeur were burned away like the morning mist. At last, he realized who was in charge—God. It was *His* dominion, *His* kingdom, *His* will, *His* works, *His* ways.

Job's Doubts

It's usually when our lives strike an iceberg and begin taking on water that we ask the questions: "Is anyone at the helm of this ship? Is anyone mapping out a destination? Is anyone on the bridge looking out for icebergs?" Such thoughts often flood our minds when calamity hits full force.

Certainly they did with Job. He lost everything but his life and his wife. And to make matters worse, as he sat covered with oozing sores, he had to endure the self-righteous counsel of his friends. No wonder he persisted in asking God: "Who's in charge around here?" Finally, God breaks His silence and reminds His servant of His sovereignty.

> Then the Lord answered Job out of the whirl-
> wind and said,
> "Who is this that darkens counsel
> By words without knowledge?
> Now gird up your loins like a man,
> And I will ask you, and you instruct Me!
> Where were you when I laid the founda-
> tion of the earth!
> Tell Me, if you have understanding,
> Who set its measurements, since you know?
> Or who stretched the line on it?
> On what were its bases sunk?
> Or who laid its cornerstone?"
> (Job 38:1–6)

Throughout chapter 38 and on into 41, God continues to ply Job with questions that lead to only one conclusion: God alone is in charge—a truth Job finally acknowledges.

> Then Job answered the Lord, and said,
> "I know that Thou canst do all things,

And that no purpose of Thine can be thwarted.
'Who is this that hides counsel without
knowledge?'
Therefore I have declared that which I did
not understand,
Things too wonderful for me, which I did
not know.
'Hear, now, and I will speak;
I will ask Thee, and do Thou instruct me.'
I have heard of Thee by the hearing of
the ear;
But now my eye sees Thee;
Therefore I retract,
And I repent in dust and ashes."
(Job 42:1–6)

In light of God's infinite wisdom and absolute power, it's hard to believe that Nebuchadnezzar could have been so filled with delusions, or Job with doubts. And yet we continually vacillate between those two extremes, don't we? When we're sailing smoothly we think we are at the helm and congratulate ourselves on our navigational skills. But when we're shipwrecked, we become inundated with doubts.

The Human Dilemma

We like to think we are free to rule our lives, that we are in charge of our destiny, masters of our fate. But such is not the case. We're free, but only to a limited extent, as A. W. Tozer so ably tells us:

> The naturalist knows that the supposedly free bird actually lives its entire life in a cage made of fears, hungers, and instincts; it is limited by weather conditions, varying air pressures, the local food supply, predatory beasts, and that strangest of all bonds, the irresistible compulsion to stay within the small plot of land and air assigned it by birdland comity. The freest bird is, along with every other created thing, held in constant check by a net of necessity. Only God is free.[1]

1. A. W. Tozer, *The Knowledge of the Holy* (New York, N.Y.: Harper and Row, Publishers, (©1961 by A. W. Tozer), pp. 115–16.

Only God is fully free. Only He exists without a rival. Only He occupies an unthreatened throne.

What Does Sovereignty Mean . . . and Not Mean?

Turning our attention now to the New Testament, we'll focus on the meaning of sovereignty as defined through the book of Romans.

What Sovereignty Does Mean

Paul's doxology in Romans 11:33–36 provides us with some key information. Let's take a closer look, beginning with verse 33.

> Oh, the depth of the riches both of the wisdom and knowledge of God! How unsearchable are His judgments and unfathomable His ways!

From this verse we can formulate this definition of sovereignty: *Our all-wise, all-knowing God reigns in realms beyond our comprehension, to bring about a plan beyond our ability to alter, hinder, or stop.* Think about it. This would include all promotions and demotions, prosperity and adversity, tragedy and ecstasy, calamity and joy. It would envelop both illness and health, danger and safety, heartache and hope. When we cannot fathom why—God knows. When we cannot give reasons—God understands. When we cannot see the end—God is there.

A. W. Tozer illustrates this point in *The Knowledge of the Holy.*

> An ocean liner leaves New York bound for Liverpool. Its destination has been determined by proper authorities. Nothing can change it. This is at least a faint picture of sovereignty.
>
> On board the liner are several scores of passengers. These are not in chains, neither are their activities determined for them by decree. They are completely free to move about as they will. They eat, sleep, play, lounge about on the deck, read, talk, altogether as they please; but all the while the great liner is carrying them steadily onward toward a predetermined port.
>
> Both freedom and sovereignty are present here and they do not contradict each other. So it is, I believe, with man's freedom and the sovereignty of God. The mighty liner of God's sovereign design

keeps its steady course over the sea of history. God moves undisturbed and unhindered toward the fulfillment of those eternal purposes which He purposed in Christ Jesus before the world began. We do not know all that is included in those purposes, but enough has been disclosed to furnish us with a broad outline of things to come and to give us good hope and firm assurance of future well-being.[2]

God's sovereignty is also not temporary or in some way limited but extends to an infinite and glorious fullness, as revealed in the rest of Paul's outpouring of praise:

For who has known the mind of the Lord, or who became His counselor? Or who has first given to Him that it might be paid back to him again? For from Him and through Him and to Him are all things. To Him be the glory forever. Amen. (vv. 34–36)

Our sovereign Lord is Master and Mover, Giver and Receiver. He is the originator, "from Him"; the enforcer, "through Him"; the provider, "to Him."

What It Does Not Mean

When this doctrine is taken to an unbiblical extreme, people allow themselves to become passive, irresponsible, and lacking in zeal as well as in personal excellence. Yet it's interesting to note the commands Paul issues immediately after his doxology in Romans 11. He urges the Romans to

- be spiritually transformed (12:1–2),

- demonstrate their spiritual gifts (vv. 6–8),

- develop loving relationships (vv. 9–21),

- and respond properly to government (13:1–7).

God's sovereignty does not release us from responsibility. And that includes the responsibility for choosing our eternal destiny. Within the scope of God's reign we have the freedom to say yes or no to Christ . . . but not the ability to change destinations once we die.

---

2. Tozer, *The Knowledge of the Holy*, p. 118.

Where Will It Lead?

Look again at Romans 11:36, focusing on the final words: "To Him be the glory forever. Amen." This is what gives sovereignty its substance. It all leads back to God's glory. He is the ultimate end, as 1 Corinthians 15:24–28 indicates.

> Then comes the end, when He delivers up the king-
> dom to the God and Father, when He has abolished
> all rule and all authority and power. For He must
> reign until He has put all His enemies under His
> feet. The last enemy that will be abolished is death.
> For He has put all things in subjection under His
> feet. But when He says, "All things are put in sub-
> jection," it is evident that He is excepted who put
> all things in subjection to Him. And when all things
> are subjected to Him, then the Son Himself also will
> be subjected to the One who subjected all things to
> Him, that God may be all in all.

"That God may be all in all." Not man. *God.* Our happiness, our reward, our blessing, our relief is not central to creation's climax—but that He may be finally acknowledged as the Most High. Deep within all our hearts whispers the persistent realization that God will have the final say.

Why Do We Care?

As we conclude this theological study, you may be wondering: "Why should I care whether God is sovereign or not? What practical difference does it make in my life?" Job answers those questions for us in chapter 42. *First,* God's sovereignty relieves us from anxiety (v. 2). *Second,* it frees us from needing an explanation (vv. 3–4). *Finally,* it keeps us from pride (vv. 5–6).

◆

God's Handwriting

He writes in characters too grand
For our short sight to understand;
We catch but broken strokes, and try
To fathom all the mystery
Of withered hopes, of death, of life,

The endless war, the useless strife—
But there, with larger, clearer sight,
We shall see this—His way was right.[3]

 Living Insights

Dr. James Dobson begins his book *When God Doesn't Make Sense* with the story of a gifted medical student named Chuck Frye. Chuck, a bright young Christian, entered the University of Arizona School of Medicine despite incredible odds—only 106 applicants were accepted out of 6,000. Chuck was on his way to a brilliant medical career. His bright future, however, began to dim as an unforeseen cloud settled over his life, bringing him face-to-face with the sovereignty of God.

> During that first term, Chuck was thinking about the call of God on his life. He began to feel that he should forgo high-tech medicine in some lucrative setting in favor of service on a foreign field. This eventually became his definite plan for the future. Toward the end of that first year of training, however, Chuck was not feeling well. He began experiencing a strange and persistent fatigue. He made an appointment for an examination in May and was soon diagnosed with acute leukemia. Chuck Frye was dead by November.[4]

Imagine the questions that gushed from Chuck's heart when he found out he was dying. And what about his parents' struggles? How, they might have wondered, could God allow the untimely death of such a gifted and devoted young man? There are other doctors, some who profit from dishonest gain, God could have taken. Why Chuck? Why now?

Why?

This question echoes through a pain-hollowed heart. And it puts its finger on one of the troubles we have with the issue of

---

3. John Oxenham, "God's Handwriting," as quoted by V. Raymond Edman, in *The Disciplines of Life* (Wheaton, Ill.: Van Kampen Press, 1948), p. 166.

4. James Dobson, *When God Doesn't Make Sense* (Wheaton, Ill.: Tyndale House Publishers, 1993), pp. 3–4.

sovereignty: *We don't know.* We don't know why, can't explain why, can't control why.

It underscores our vulnerability, forcing us to face the truth that we live in an uncertain world where bad things often happen to good people. And it's hard to live with the uncertain and unknown, isn't it?

God is in control, and frankly, there is no way we can understand all that that means. It's not a simple panacea for every pain.

Yes, God is in control, but we are not. Our wholehearted belief in God's sovereignty doesn't guarantee we'll know *why*. We believe God, but we are *not* God.

So sometimes maybe the best we can do is to be honest about our vulnerable limitedness . . . and admit that we don't fully understand our sovereign, righteous, limitless Lord (see Isa. 55:8–9).

 Living Insights

> Becky Diener sat upstairs in her bedroom and looked at the tree. She was stuck on an assignment from Miss Melrose for English, a 750-word personal essay, "Describe your backyard as if you were seeing it for the first time." After an hour she had thirty-nine words, which she figured would mean she'd finish at 1:45 P.M. Tuesday, four hours late, and therefore would get an F even if the essay was great, which it certainly wasn't.
>
> How can you describe your backyard as if you'd never seen it? If you'd never seen it, you'd have grown up someplace else, and wouldn't be yourself; you'd be someone else entirely, and how are you supposed to know what that person would think?[5]

Becky Diener, one of many characters created by Garrison Keillor for his Lake Wobegon stories, has a dilemma: How do you appreciate something as familiar as your own backyard; something that's always there, whether you notice it or not? A steady, unobtrusive part of life's landscape. Her pen would have flowed with ease for a more exquisite topic, such as the canals of Venice or the Swiss Alps. What does a backyard have to offer?

5. Garrison Keillor, *Leaving Home: A Collection of Lake Wobegon Stories* (New York, N.Y.: Viking Penguin, 1987), p. 49.

9

But as Becky stared at the crab apple tree, memories of her childhood began to blossom. She remembered planting the little sapling in the dirt with her father. She recalled the story of her parents' courtship and marriage—how Harold proposed to Marlys with a bouquet of flowering crab apple. How Dad twisted his ankle jumping off the garage to impress the kids. How he tended the tree until it grew to sprout purple blossoms each spring.

She finished her assignment, having gained a new appreciation for the old tree and her very normal backyard.

> It's the most magnificent thing in the Dieners' backyard. Becky finished writing 750 words late that night and lay down to sleep. A backyard is a novel about us, and when we sit there on a summer day, we hear the dialogue and see the characters.[6]

How long has it been since you savored the flowering beauty of God's sovereignty? Sometimes we take it for granted. We know it's out there, standing firm as ever in our theological backyard. But we don't stop at the window long enough to appreciate its grandeur.

Take a moment to sit in front of your life's window and look at God's sovereignty as if you were seeing it for the first time. Does it bring back memories? Whom did He provide to tell you about salvation in Christ? How has He protected you and your family? What has He taught you in the classroom of adversity? What good things has He given you that you thought you didn't need? What harmful things has He withheld that you desperately wanted? Let your mind wander. Write down your thoughts, and let God's sovereignty become the "most magnificent thing" in your backyard.

_____

_____

_____

_____

_____

_____

_____

6. Keillor, *Leaving Home*, p. 54.

Chapter 2

GOD'S MERCY
Selected Scriptures

T he novel *Les Misérables* was written by the highly acclaimed French author Victor Hugo in the mid-1800s. Set during the French revolution, it is the story of Jean Valjean, a man who nineteen years earlier had been sentenced to hard labor on a chain gang for stealing bread to feed his sister's starving daughter.

He is one of "the miserable," and even though he's finally paroled, he is looked on as an outcast, condemned to a life of poverty and shame.

Only the saintly bishop of Digne treats him kindly and takes him into his home to feed and shelter him. But Valjean, embittered by years of hardship, repays the bishop's kindness by stealing his silverware. Later, he is caught by the police and dragged back to the bishop to return the stolen goods before being sent back to prison.

To Valjean's astonishment, though, the bishop covers his crime, telling the police that the silverware was a gift. And along with the silverware, the bishop gives Valjean two precious candlesticks as well.

This act of mercy not only keeps Valjean out of prison but gives him the strength to start a new life—a life of kindness and compassion to others.

Few stories illustrate the profound impact mercy can have on a person better than *Les Misérables*. In our lesson today, we will examine this incredible life-changing ministry of God.

A Definition of Mercy

Mercy isn't mere pity, understanding, or sorrow; it is divine action on behalf of offenders and victims whereby God brings relief. To give a formal definition: *Mercy is God's inexhaustible and infinite compassion, which He demonstrates to the miserable* (compare Eph. 2:1–7, especially v. 4). Probably no one is a greater example of the life-changing effects of mercy than the apostle Paul.

> I thank Christ Jesus our Lord, who has strengthened me, because He considered me faithful, putting me into service; even though I was formerly a blasphemer and a persecutor and a violent aggressor.

And yet I was shown mercy, because I acted ignorantly in unbelief. (1 Tim. 1:12–13)

The gentle rain of God's mercy didn't stop with biblical days, however. With each generation God's mercy falls on parched human hearts; and where it falls, life sprouts anew. It did for John Newton, author of the hymn "Amazing Grace." In his self-composed epitaph he wrote:

> "John Newton, Clerk, once an Infidel and Libertine, a Servant of Slaves in Africa, was by the Mercy of our Lord and Saviour Jesus Christ, Preserved, Restored, Pardoned, and Appointed to Preach the Faith he had so long laboured to destroy."[1]

Some Biblical Illustrations

Turning back to the Old Testament, we find that one Hebrew word for *mercy* stands out—*chesed*. Often it's translated "kindness" or "lovingkindness." As we trace the term through the Old Testament, we see at least five different miseries to which it brings relief.

Suffering the Consequences of Unfair Treatment

Falsely accused of raping Potiphar's wife, Joseph is imprisoned (Gen. 39). Yet in the midst of this unjust treatment, God is there as a pillow of grace in the hard circumstances upon which Joseph is forced to lay his head.

> But the Lord was with Joseph and extended *kindness* to him, and gave him favor in the sight of the chief jailer. And the chief jailer committed to Joseph's charge all the prisoners who were in the jail; so that whatever was done there, he was responsible for it. The chief jailer did not supervise anything under Joseph's charge because the Lord was with him; and whatever he did, the Lord made to prosper. (vv. 21–23, emphasis added)

---

1. John Newton, as quoted by William Barclay, in *The Letters to Timothy, Titus, and Philemon*, rev. ed., The Daily Study Bible Series (Philadelphia, Pa.: Westminster Press, 1975), p. 46.

Enduring Grief after the Loss of a Loved One

Newly widowed, Naomi welcomed the marriages of her two sons to Orpah and Ruth. Then tragedy struck, and both sons died (Ruth 1:5). But Naomi's comforting words to her daughters-in-law include the assurance of *chesed*—mercy.

> "Go, return each of you to her mother's house. May the Lord deal *kindly* with you as you have dealt with the dead and with me. May the Lord grant that you may find rest, each in the house of her husband." Then she kissed them, and they lifted up their voices and wept. (vv. 8–9, emphasis added)

Struggling with the Limitations of a Disability

Second Samuel 9 tells the story of an overlooked crippled man named Mephibosheth, a descendant of Saul, the late king of Israel (vv. 1–13). King David seeks out the man—who trembles in his presence, for the ancient kings of the east used to annihilate the descendants of the kings they succeeded. But David allays his fears with an extraordinary demonstration of kindness.

> "Do not fear, for I will surely show *kindness* to you for the sake of your father Jonathan, and will restore to you all the land of your grandfather Saul; and you shall eat at my table regularly." (v. 7, emphasis added)

Hurting Physically

Probably no example of prolonged physical agony stands out in the Scriptures as sharply as Job's. He was blighted with sores without and beleaguered with questions within. And in the ash heap of those unanswered questions, he sat in disgrace. In fact, "sated with disgrace" is how he described himself in Job 10:15. And yet, in the midst of almost overwhelming pain, he could say:

> "'Thou hast granted me life and *lovingkindness*;
> And Thy care has preserved my spirit.'"
> (v. 12, emphasis added)

Bearing the Guilt of Transgression

Probably the most miserable pain we can find ourselves in is not physical but spiritual. Psalm 32:3–5 describes the misery of those who keep their sins secret from God.

When I kept silent about my sin, my body wasted
        away
Through my groaning all day long.
For day and night Thy hand was heavy upon me;
My vitality was drained away as with the fever
        heat of summer.
I acknowledged my sin to Thee,
And my iniquity I did not hide;
I said, "I will confess my transgressions to the Lord";
And Thou didst forgive the guilt of my sin.

And yet, even in our most disgraceful fall into sin, God is there
to extend a merciful hand to help us up, dust us off, and get us on
our feet again.

Many are the sorrows of the wicked;
But he who trusts in the Lord, *lovingkindness* shall
        surround him. (v. 10, emphasis added)

In Psalm 23:6, David expresses his trust in God's *chesed:* "Surely
goodness and mercy shall follow me all the days of my life" (KJV).
And it is this characteristic of God that David clings to after his
sin with Bathsheba:

Be gracious to me, O God, according to Thy
        lovingkindness;
According to the greatness of Thy compassion
        blot out my transgressions.
(51:1, emphasis added)

For the fallen, mercy is waiting to tenderly embrace the con-
fessor. Mercy we can depend on to be there. Always.

Mercy at Work Theologically

Mercy is always wrapped in tenderness. In the Old Testament,
when the tabernacle was built, God arranged for a box—the ark
of the covenant—to be kept in the holiest place of all. Set behind
a thick veil, it contained the Ten Commandments and Aaron's rod.
Over the tablets of stone there was a little lid exactly in the shape
of the altar. Over this lid and altar were two golden angels called
cherubim, one on each side, looking onto the "mercy seat," or altar.
This was the most intimate place in the tabernacle—the place
where the blood of sacrifices was poured out century after century.

It's called the mercy seat because when the blood covers the Law, while the cherubim watch, God is satisfied and His anger is abated. How symbolic that God would choose a small lid over an ark watched by silent, golden cherubim as the place where He would commune with His people. It wasn't a place of Law, it was a place of mercy.

Mercy at Work Personally

Remember, mercy gives relief to the miserable. It's both intensely personal and immensely practical. For when I am treated unfairly, God's mercy relieves my bitterness . . . when I grieve over loss, it relieves my pain and anger and denial . . . when I struggle with a disability, it relieves my self-pity . . . when I endure physical pain, it relieves my hopelessness . . . when I deal with sinful actions, it relieves my guilt.

The film *Tender Mercies* is about two opposites who marry. He is a man battling with alcohol, bitter over a lost career as a country-western musician. She's a widow whose husband was killed in Vietnam. She never makes enormous demands on him, never threatens him, never expects too much.

Quietly . . . graciously . . . patiently . . . with tender mercy, she trusts God to deal with her husband.

The story comes to a climax when the husband, in the throes of depression, buys a bottle and peels out in his pickup. Meanwhile, his wife waits in bed, quoting Scripture to encourage herself while he's gone. Finally, he returns, telling her, "I bought a bottle, but I poured it out. I didn't drink anything."

His life turns a corner at this point. And he goes back to the work he once loved—songwriting.

Tender mercies—that's what God uses to change lives.

———◆———

Dear Father,

May we all become people more like God, people of mercy. When we see those who are in need, when we ourselves are in need, may we become people of mercy. Like the widow in the movie, may we lessen our demands and increase our compassion, just as our God does with us.

Thank You, Father, for Your many tender mercies. How greatly we need them. And all through this week, may we worship You between those golden wings where mercy sits and waits for us. In the name of Jesus Christ we pray. Amen.

 Living Insights

"I pardon you, I pardon you. I pardon you too." Amon Goeth seemed to enjoy this new kind of power. After putting countless Jews to death in his work camp, the German officer appeared refreshed by the change in routine. His impulsive mercy, however, took the Jews by surprise. By now they had come to expect execution for the smallest infraction—a miscalculation in construction, failure to meet production quotas, standing in the wrong place at the wrong time.

Perhaps Schindler's words lodged somewhere in Goeth's icy heart and started a slow thaw. Oskar Schindler, a German entrepreneur who eventually rescued hundreds of Jews from extermination, tried to convince Goeth that real power resides in mercy, not judgment. To possess the means and authority to enact judgment and choose not to use it—that's power indeed.

But the thrill died, and so did more Jews. After a young boy failed to scour all the grime from Goeth's tub, the officer released him with a disdainful "I pardon you." Then from the balcony of his chalet, he shot the boy with a scoped rifle. For Goeth, the pleasure of dispensing mercy was short-lived.

Though most of us would never dream of committing the atrocities portrayed in the movie *Schindler's List*, we often enjoy wielding a hammer of judgment more than offering a tender hand of mercy. "Give them what they have coming" is usually our first thought. But mercy demands more of us. Mercy releases bitterness, harbors no grudges, keeps no score.

Unlike Amon Goeth, Christians possess the Holy Spirit, who transforms us into mercy-givers as we depend on Him. Which do you dole out more often? Mercy or judgment? If it's judgment, here's a suggestion that might provide some balance.

Write down the names of two people who need to receive your mercy this week. Perhaps a subordinate at the office hasn't heard your approval or encouragement for a while. Maybe you need to release your spouse and children from unreasonable expectations. Is there someone sick you can call or visit? Someone lonely you can invite to dinner? Someone guilty you can forgive? Mercy can be expressed in a thousand ways. See if you can come up with two. Then ask God for opportunities to radiate His mercy to these people.

How I can demonstrate mercy to _____ :

_____

_____

_____

How I can demonstrate mercy to _____ :

_____

_____

_____

Living Insights   STUDY TWO

Remember John Newton's self-composed epitaph?

> "John Newton, Clerk, once an Infidel and Libertine, a Servant of Slaves in Africa, was by the Mercy of our Lord and Saviour Jesus Christ, Preserved, Restored, Pardoned, and Appointed to Preach the Faith he had so long laboured to destroy."

The light of God's mercy pierced the darkness of John Newton's heart. And like the apostle Paul, he never stopped glowing. How about you? Do you still radiate with the glow of God's mercy? Do you still marvel that His tender hand intervened to alter your course? Do you remember how you were before Jesus Christ entered your life?

If you've never written your own epitaph, give it a try. Only two criteria: (1) Keep it under fifty words, and (2) make it a record of God's mercy in your life. When you're finished, use the epitaph as a springboard to prayer and praise to God.

My epitaph of mercy: _____

_____

_____

Chapter 3
GOD'S FAITHFULNESS
Lamentations 3:19–32

For many of us entrenched in dieting's "battle of the bulge," it's the bulge that usually wins. We may start early Monday morning, determined to trim off the fat. But by Wednesday we've begun to compromise. And when Friday comes we're back to our old habits. Perhaps that's why we relate so well to the "stress diet":

Breakfast: one-half grapefruit
one piece of whole wheat toast—
no butter
eight ounces of skim milk
coffee—black

Lunch: four ounces of lean, broiled chicken
breast—skin removed
one cup of steamed zucchini
herb tea—no sugar
one Oreo cookie

Snack: the rest of the package of Oreo cookies
one quart rocky road ice cream
one jar of hot fudge

Dinner: two loaves of garlic bread—heavy on
the butter
one large sausage and pepperoni
pizza—extra cheese
two large milk shakes with whipped
cream
and for dessert, three Milky Way
candy bars and an entire frozen
cheesecake

Oh, the impact of one Oreo cookie!

Compromises complicate our commitments. They may be funny in a ridiculous diet such as this one. But compromises are tragic when they bring down a nation.

One wonders when Israel ate that first cookie. Maybe it was when one family first found a Canaanite idol. They didn't worship it. They just decided to toss it in the closet. No big deal. After all, it was only a wood carving. It meant nothing to them. But then one of the children discovered it, or maybe a neighbor was curious, and before they knew it, one compromise led to another. Before they realized it, Israel not only sampled the Canaanites' Oreo, but they ended up swallowing the whole package as well.

> With their silver and gold they have made idols for
>   themselves. . . .
> They sow the wind
> And they reap the whirlwind. (Hos. 8:4b, 7a)

What may have begun as the cherishing of a little artifact ended up as a massive manufacturing effort that led the nation away from God and into wholesale idolatry. Benjamin Franklin, back in 1758, pictured compromise's far-reaching effects: "A little neglect may breed great mischief . . . for want of a nail the shoe was lost; for want of a shoe the horse was lost; and for want of a horse the rider was lost."[1]

Now is the time to pay attention to the nail, to take a look at the cookie, because neglecting these details is the first step down to defeat. For when we continue doing wrong, we set in motion a cycle of catastrophic complications.

A Cycle Regularly Repeated

In 722 B.C., the Assyrians invaded the northern kingdom of Israel and took the Jews of that region into captivity. Then in 586 B.C., the Babylonian army swarmed over Jerusalem, took the southern kingdom captive, and marched the people of Judah off to Babylon. God's people were indeed swept away by the whirlwind.

The prophet Jeremiah watched this upheaval and prophesied for forty tearful years. In his journal, titled The Lamentations of Jeremiah, he recorded what he saw and felt after the fall of Judah. *Lament* means "a crying out in grief."[2] It's a wailing cry in the middle of the night. It's the sadness brought on by loss. As Jeremiah stumbled through the rubble of Zion, he took notes and remembered with aching heart the days when his nation was great.

---

1. Benjamin Franklin, as quoted in *Bartlett's Familiar Quotations*, 15th ed., rev. and enl., ed. Emily Morison Beck (Boston, Mass.: Little, Brown and Co., 1980), p. 347.

2. *Merriam-Webster's Collegiate Dictionary*, 10th ed., see "lament."

I am the man who has seen affliction
Because of the rod of His wrath.
He has driven me and made me walk
In darkness and not in light.
Surely against me He has turned His hand
Repeatedly all the day. (Lam. 3:1–3)

Israel had deliberately, consciously, and with some sense of calculation walked away from the ways of God. Now His afflicting whirlwind was beginning to sweep the people off their feet. That's when affliction turns to desolation. Look at verses 8–11.

Even when I cry out and call for help,
He shuts out my prayer.
He has blocked my ways with hewn stone;
He has made my paths crooked.
He is to me like a bear lying in wait,
Like a lion in secret places.
He has turned aside my ways and torn me to pieces;
He has made me desolate.

In desolation, the people fall helpless on their backs. Isolated, they feel rejected by God. Then comes mockery from others, and with it, humiliation.

I have become a laughingstock to all my people,
Their mocking song all the day. (v. 14)

Jeremiah records it all in his journal: He is "broken" (v. 4); He is "blocked" (v. 9); He is "bitter" (v. 15). His desolate heart even forgets what happiness is (v. 17). Like the branches of a tree in a violent storm, the prophet's spirit is bowed within him (v. 20). Yet when he looks up, he sees the character of God standing firm. It doesn't sway, and that changes his perspective on the storm.

A Passage Worth Remembering

The hinge in Jeremiah's thinking is verse 21.

This I recall to my mind,
Therefore I have hope.

Hope. The human body can live forty days without food, maybe eight days without water, only a few minutes without air. But the human spirit can't live for more than a few seconds without hope.

Jeremiah has been walking through the remains of the city he loves, kicking the debris, remembering the bitterness, and wondering how all this could have happened. Suddenly, three shining truths dawn on his darkened heart.

> The Lord's lovingkindnesses indeed never cease. (v. 22a)

Note the plural form—it shows that many are God's loving-kindnesses, His mercies. We need to have this truth blazed into our brains: *The Lord's mercies never cease.*

Aren't you glad God isn't fickle? Aren't you glad that, even when you run, His mercy stays? We are the sheep of His own pasture, and His goodness and mercy follow us all the days of our lives (see Ps. 23:6). They *never* cease.

The next word of hope is found in the second part of Jeremiah's verse:

> For His compassions never fail. (Lam. 3:22b)

The Lord's compassions never fail. The word *compassion* means "sympathetic love, concern for the helpless." In reference to God, it always includes involvement, and it is always unalterably the same. Like the father in Luke 15, God keeps loving His prodigal children. Remember the story?

The younger son wants his inheritance so he can leave home and see the world. The father doesn't run after him and plead with him or promise him more money. He lets him go, just as our Father lets us. Eventually, the boy runs out of money and food. And finally, in a pigsty, he comes to his senses. When he returns home, the father doesn't shame him or reject him or interrogate him. No, he runs to meet his son, showers him with hugs and kisses, restores his sonship, and throws a jubilant party in his honor. He has compassion on him (see v. 20).

How much more do our Father's compassions remain open and waiting for us!

Back in Lamentations 3:23, another ray of hope pierces through the dark clouds hovering over Jerusalem.

> They are new every morning;
> Great is Thy faithfulness.

Even when we blow it. Even when we make stupid decisions. Even when our marriages fail or our businesses go bankrupt. Even when we know better. *The Lord's faithfulness never diminishes.* It is always, always great. And it is new every morning.

What is God's morning message to us? The dawn itself.

It doesn't matter whether the sky is clear and bright, cloudy and rainy. He says *every morning,* not just when the sun shines. Every morning the Lord sends the message: "I'm still here. Let's go through the day together. Tomorrow we'll face tomorrow. But for today, I'm here to faithfully show you love, kindness, and compassion."

And because of His unchanging character, His faithfulness will remain unconditional, unending, unswerving. Now there's a reason to face another day . . . and face it with hope.

A Suggestion Worth Trying

Right now, in the nearness of this present moment, trust God to remember you. He's faithful to know not only who you are but where you are—where you're running from, and where you're running to. And all the while He's dogging your heels with His untiring faithfulness. He's there and He cares. How do we trust Him? In verses 24–32, God gives us four ways to carry out our trust.

Wait patiently. Stop running and start waiting. In verse 25 Jeremiah assures us, "The Lord is good to those who wait for Him." Trust Him to remember His goodness toward you . . . by waiting on His unchanging faithfulness.

Seek diligently. Instead of ignoring Him, start seeking Him again. Confess your wrongs, uncover your shame before Him, and come to Him on the merits of Christ. For the Lord is good "to the person who seeks Him" (v. 25b).

Sit silently. "Let him sit alone and be silent Since He has laid it on him" (v. 28). After you've poured out your heart to God, be quiet. Try spending a day in solitude. Take a passage, a psalm, a section of Scripture that's meaningful to you and let it speak. Say nothing; just sit quietly. Let Him talk. Let Him reassure you. Feel His arms around you. Understand the cleansing that He's bringing and the freshness of His presence.

Submit willingly. When circumstances are standing over you with their foot on your neck, the tendency is to want to stand up and defend yourself. But Jeremiah advises just the opposite.

> Let him put his mouth in the dust,
> Perhaps there is hope.
> Let him give his cheek to the smiter;

Let him be filled with reproach. (vv. 29–30)

This means no rationalizing, no excuses. Stop trying to get around the heinous sin in your life. Face it. Submissively. Willingly. If you do, verses 31–32 offer a wonderful promise of encouragement.

> For the Lord will not reject forever,
> For if He causes grief,
> Then He will have compassion
> According to His abundant lovingkindness.

If you wait patiently, seek God diligently, sit silently, and submit willingly, He will show you that His mercies haven't ceased, His compassions haven't failed, and His faithfulness hasn't diminished.

◆

> *Great is Thy faithfulness, O God my Father!*
> *There is no shadow of turning with Thee;*
> *Thou changest not, Thy compassions, they fail not: As*
> *Thou hast been Thou forever wilt be.*
>
> *Great is Thy faithfulness,*
> *Great is Thy faithfulness,*
> *Morning by morning new mercies I see;*
> *All I have needed Thy hand hath provided—*
> *Great is Thy faithfulness, Lord, unto me!*[3]

 Living Insights

Have you ever felt as though God didn't love you? That some of the things you do or say hinder His love's flow like a clogged pipe? That your spiritual warts make God wince when He looks your direction?

Most of us are skilled at controlling the amount of love we give. We keep our hand on the valve, ready to start or stop the gush at a moment's notice—depending on how we're treated. But God's love never runs dry. His faithfulness keeps the reservoir infinitely full and endlessly flowing. In fact, Paul tells us in Romans that

---

3. Thomas O. Chisholm, "Great Is Thy Faithfulness," in *Hymns for the Family of God* (Nashville, Tenn.: Paragon Associates, 1976), no. 98.

nothing can separate us from the love of God.

If you've done something lately that you feel might cause God to disown you, spend a few minutes in Romans 8:38–39. Do you see anything there that might stop God from loving you?

God's love never fails. It doesn't depend on how we feel or what goes wrong. It depends on who He is. And He is faithful.

> The Lord's lovingkindnesses indeed never cease,
> For His compassions never fail.
> They are new every morning;
> Great is Thy faithfulness. (Lam. 3:22)

 ## *Living Insights*

Southern California: Sun-baked beaches caressed by whispering waves. Towering palm trees. Windswept patios and outdoor cafes. Rugged mountains. Movie stars. And smog.

Smog. It lingers in the Los Angeles Basin like an obese ghost. Fat and lazy from an undisciplined diet of exhaust fumes, it rolls over on rare occasions to allow a glimpse of the mountains. On most days, though, one must take it by faith that the peaks are there, obscured by a slothful spirit who cares more about sleep than scenery.

Walking with God is sometimes like looking for a concealed mountain, isn't it? We know He's there, that He's faithful. But spiritual smog—bloated with emotional and physical pain, relational strain, even sin—hides Him from view. So we walk by faith, knowing that murky circumstances can't weaken God's faithfulness any more than smog can tear down a mountain range. But a glimpse of Him would be nice.

How long has it been since you asked your Heavenly Father to clear away the smog and reveal Himself to you? Why don't you try that now. Don't expect all your problems to disappear, but ask God to encourage you with His presence. Take along a Scripture passage or two (Psalm 139 is a great one). Get alone. Be quiet and seek God. Love Him. Thank Him. Ask of Him. Confess to Him.

Enjoy the view.

Chapter 4

GOD'S HOLINESS

Selected Scriptures

Reading through 1 and 2 Kings is like walking through a royal graveyard. The stories of Israel's rulers read like brief epitaphs etched in marble headstones—until we come to Uzziah's. Many of the kings served only a few years, some just a few months. But Uzziah ruled over Israel for fifty-two years. So established was this king's reign that the people faced the danger of placing him on the pedestal of their hearts and thus dethroning their true king, the Lord God.

Perhaps Isaiah had his eyes on Uzziah too, and not on God. Maybe that's why the Lord got the prophet's attention one day by revealing Himself.

> In the year of King Uzziah's death, I saw the Lord sitting on a throne, lofty and exalted, with the train of His robe filling the temple. Seraphim stood above Him, each having six wings; with two he covered his face, and with two he covered his feet, and with two he flew. And one called out to another and said,
> "Holy, Holy, Holy, is the Lord of hosts,
> The whole earth is full of His glory."
> And the foundations of the thresholds trembled at the voice of him who called out, while the temple was filling with smoke. (Isa. 6:1–4)

When Isaiah saw himself in contrast to the unspeakable glory of God, he realized his true condition.

> "Woe is me, for I am ruined!
> Because I am a man of unclean lips,
> And I live among a people of unclean lips;
> For my eyes have seen the King, the Lord of hosts."
> (v. 5)

God's holiness is a transforming truth—and a subject well worth our attention.

An Understanding of Holiness

Both the Hebrew and Greek words for *holy* convey the idea of separateness. When Scripture says something is holy, it means it is set apart—dedicated or consecrated for the work and glory of God. For instance, a piece of furniture may be dedicated for use in a sanctuary or a robe might be consecrated for use by a minister. In reference to behavior, holiness means separation from all that is sinful, impure, and imperfect. This is one of God's essential characteristics—He is completely free of contamination.

Although God offers us complete forgiveness, in this life we can never experience the holiness of a completely sinless existence because of our fallen condition. That's why Isaiah responded as he did to God's glory. We can better understand his feelings by imagining ourselves caked with mud, dressed in filthy rags, and then stepping into the scrubbed, gleaming, stainless steel sterility of a hospital operating room. Those high-wattage surgical lamps would spotlight our grimy faces the way God's glory shone on Isaiah's dirty soul.

A Realization of Its Importance

Why do we need to know about God's holiness? Because of what it reveals about God and how it affects us.

What It Reveals about God

First, God's holiness assures us that He is trustworthy; He is morally unable to take advantage of us, abuse us, or manipulate us. We can trust Him to do what is right by us at all times.

Second, His holiness guarantees that He will deal honorably with us; we will never have to wonder whether His plans will backfire or work against us. His holy will is free of question.

Third, since He is holy, He is our model of perfection—He is without flaw, either hidden or exposed.[1]

---

1. James 1:13 says: "Let no one say when he is tempted, 'I am being tempted by God'; for God cannot be tempted by evil, and He Himself does not tempt anyone." In this passage there is a unique construction in the original text that highlights the intricate and infinite holiness of God. It's in the phrase, "I am being tempted by God." This particular construction conveys the idea of indirect agency; namely, that God is not even *indirectly* involved in the act of sin.

How It Affects Us

What if God reserved holiness only for Himself, withholding that quality from us? Well, first, we would not be able to fellowship with Him.

> And this is the message we have heard from Him
> and announce to you, that God is light, and in Him
> there is no darkness at all. If we say that we have
> fellowship with Him and yet walk in the darkness,
> we lie and do not practice the truth. (1 John 1:5–6)

The word *light* is being used as a symbol of purity. God is absolutely pure, with not one dark thought, not one stained motive, not one shady statement or act. It is impossible for light to coexist with darkness, for holiness to coexist with sin. But through His grace, God gives us the opportunity to overcome the darkness of our souls and walk in the light of His holiness:

> If we walk in the light as He Himself is in the light,
> we have fellowship with one another, and the blood
> of Jesus His Son cleanses us from all sin. (v. 7)

Second, without holiness, not only would we be separated from God, but we'd live our entire lives in the stranglehold of sin, unable to free ourselves from its grip. Like Isaiah, we could only cry, "Woe is me, for I am ruined!" We'd have no hope.

And third, without holiness, we would never see our Lord, as Hebrews 12:14 tells us:

> Pursue peace with all men, and the *sanctification*
> without which no one will see the Lord. (emphasis
> added)

The Greek term is *hagiasmos*, which has at its root the word for *holy, hagios*. Without holiness being transferred to our account through the righteousness of God, we would have no promise of heaven.

As excellent and vital as holiness is, it can still feel spooky and ethereal, can't it? How can holiness possibly be achieved by sinful humans? The mysteriousness of it is magnified by two conflicting approaches. One says that we can never work hard enough, never give up enough to achieve holiness. The other says that holiness is all up to God, that we're just passive recipients who have no involvement in the process of becoming holy people.

Neither of these is very helpful—or accurate. So let's set aside human reasoning and see instead what the Holy One Himself has said in His Word.

A Few Examples from Scripture

Two thoughts rise to the surface when we examine holiness in the Scriptures. First, holiness always suggests separateness and differentness. God, being holy, is different and separate from all other gods. So, if we plan to form our lives in God's holiness, we, too, must be marked by a sense of separation and difference.

And second, holiness is always connected with moral excellence and ethical beauty. To be holy as God is holy, then, means that we emulate His morality. Immorality and holiness, like oil and water, don't mix.

Let's turn now to the palette of Scripture and see the brilliant hues God uses to portray true holiness.

In the Old Testament

Leviticus 11 shows that we aren't merely to sit back and admire God's holiness, but we're to actively be distinct and morally pure as He is.

> "'For I am the Lord your God. Consecrate yourselves therefore, and be holy; for I am holy. And you shall not make yourselves unclean with any of the swarming things that swarm on the earth. For I am the Lord, who brought you up from the land of Egypt, to be your God; thus you shall be holy for I am holy.'" (vv. 44–45)

Our active involvement is further highlighted in Psalm 24.

> Who may ascend into the hill of the Lord?
> And who may stand in His holy place?
> He who has clean hands and a pure heart,
> Who has not lifted up his soul to falsehood,
> And has not sworn deceitfully.
> He shall receive a blessing from the Lord
> And righteousness from the God of his salvation.
> (vv. 3–5)

How practical the Lord is! Not one word of self-flagellation or

Spartan denial of needs is recommended here; instead, the requirements for approaching our holy God are a clean heart and a truthful tongue.

Isaiah 52:10 balances our involvement with God's holy strength, which guides and guards us through our journey on this earth.

> The Lord has bared His holy arm
> In the sight of all the nations,
> That all the ends of the earth may see
> The salvation of our God.

In the New Testament

Over in the New Testament, we find the roles that personal responsibility and grace play in a life of holiness.

> Therefore do not let sin reign in your mortal body that you should obey its lusts, and do not go on presenting the members of your body to sin as instruments of unrighteousness; but present yourselves to God as those alive from the dead, and your members as instruments of righteousness to God. For sin shall not be master over you, for you are not under law, but under grace.
>
> What then? Shall we sin because we are not under law but under grace? May it never be! Do you not know that when you present yourselves to someone as slaves for obedience, you are slaves of the one whom you obey, either of sin resulting in death, or of obedience resulting in righteousness? But thanks be to God that though you were slaves of sin, you became obedient from the heart to that form of teaching to which you were committed, and having been freed from sin, you became slaves of righteousness. (Rom. 6:12–18)

Without Christ, we are slaves to the harsh taskmaster of sin. We can make all the resolutions we wish, but we cannot keep from serving sin unless we have a power that overcomes it for us. That power is Christ.

When we come to the Cross, our slavery to sin is canceled, and we become enslaved to God. Yet sin still dwells within us—not as a landlord but as a tenant. When we invite Christ to be master of our hearts, the title is transferred from sin to the Savior. And like the new owner of an old fixer-upper, Christ sweeps our hearts clean of any dirty deeds, dusty thoughts, and cobwebs of deceit.

Though the old landlord continually tries to reclaim the property, and though we're often tempted to let him, we've been given the power to keep him under lock and key. For with our salvation we were given justification, peace, and a new capacity for holiness. First Corinthians 3:16–17 even describes us as temples of the Holy Spirit.

> Do you not know that you are a temple of God, and that the Spirit of God dwells in you? If any man destroys the temple of God, God will destroy him, for the temple of God is holy, and that is what you are.

First Thessalonians 4:3–7 describes the housekeeping chores delegated to us as caretakers of His temple.

> For this is the will of God, your sanctification; that is, that you abstain from sexual immorality; that each of you know how to possess his own vessel in sanctification and honor, not in lustful passion, like the Gentiles who do not know God; and that no man transgress and defraud his brother in the matter because the Lord is the avenger in all these things, just as we also told you before and solemnly warned you. For God has not called us for the purpose of impurity, but in sanctification.

Peter echoes Paul's admonition with five active commands in 1 Peter 1:13–16:

- first, prepare your minds for action;

- second, be self-controlled;

- third, fix your hope completely on the grace of Jesus Christ;

- fourth, do not be conformed to your former lusts;

- and fifth, in all you do, be holy as God is holy.

Nowhere in these passages do we find the phrase, "let go and let God." The only letting go we are commanded to do is the letting go of former lusts. Throughout Scripture, the Christian life is described as a battle (see Eph. 6:10–18). And there's nothing passive about a soldier in battle. God indeed empowers us (see 2 Pet. 1:4). But we fight the fight (see vv. 5–11; 2 Tim. 4:7).

In Light of What We Have Heard . . .

If we want to stand unashamed in the light of God's holiness, there are three things for us to do continually. First, we need *to keep ourselves from conforming to former lusts* (1 Pet. 1:14), remembering to claim God's power as we lock those things out of our lives. Second, we must *remind ourselves of our calling.* He who has called us is holy, and He has called us to share in that holiness (vv. 15–16). Third, we need *to conduct ourselves in fear,* as verse 17 reveals:

> If you address as Father the One who impartially judges according to each man's work, conduct yourselves in fear during the time of your stay upon earth.

This verse doesn't mean fear as in terror, but fear as in reverence— an awe-inspiring recognition of God's holiness and purity.

◆

Worship the Lord in the Beauty of Holiness

Worship the Lord in the beauty of holiness,
Bow down before Him, His glory proclaim;
Gold of obedience, and incense of lowliness,
Kneel and adore Him,—the Lord is His name. . . .

Truth in its beauty, and love in its tenderness,
These are the offerings we lay on His shrine;
These, though we bring them in trembling
and fearfulness,
He will accept in the Name all divine.[2]

 Living Insights

Having basked in the light of God's holiness, let's take a good, hard look at ourselves. Have we been neglecting the dust when it

---

2. John S. B. Monsell, "Worship the Lord in the Beauty of Holiness," in *Masterpieces of Religious Verse,* ed. James Dalton Morrison (New York, N.Y.: Harper and Brothers Publishers, 1948), p. 114, stanzas 1 and 3.

comes to our own heart's holiness? Have we been indifferent about the cobwebs in the corners of our lives? Are the rugs of our hearts lumpy from years of dirt being swept under them?

The Lord first entered our hearts when they were dusty and disheveled. When He did, He condemned the tenement slums that stood there and consecrated them as temples. Isn't it time for all of us to do some industrial-strength housecleaning?

Which rooms in your spiritual house would you like the Holy Spirit to clean up? Spend a few minutes in prayer, asking the Spirit of God to reveal areas of personal unholiness. Thank God that He loves you anyway, then jot down your discoveries.

_____

_____

_____

Now choose one to focus on this week. Commit it to prayer every morning when you rise. You may even want to write down what you are asking for specifically, leaving some room to record how God answers your prayers.

_____

_____

_____

_____

_____

_____

Don't despair if this messy area isn't spick-and-span overnight; it may be a long-term project. But our holy, righteous Lord never tires of housecleaning.

 Living Insights STUDY TWO

Sovereignty. Mercy. Faithfulness. Holiness. Four wonderful attributes of God, each with the potential to change our lives. What did you experience as you worked through each chapter?

Did the Lord's sovereignty bring reassurance to your anxious heart? Humility to a prideful life? Did His mercy touch a place of misery with relief and hope? How about His faithfulness? Did it put a kinder, more trustworthy face on your image of God? And what comfort or challenge did bowing before His holiness bring?

Take time to write down and remember the new mercies you've seen in this study, as well as the direction for the future they've inspired in you.

God's Sovereignty _____

_____

_____

God's Mercy _____

_____

_____

God's Faithfulness _____

_____

_____

God's Holiness _____

_____

_____

BOOKS FOR
PROBING FURTHER

"I shall remember the deeds of the Lord," the psalmist wrote, "Surely I will remember Thy wonders of old" (Ps. 77:11). Has this series recalled to your mind the Lord's ancient "wonders"— those timeless acts that radiate the splendor of His marvelous character? We hope so. And we also hope that these scenes "of old" have given you a new window through which to view His sovereignty, mercy, faithfulness, and holiness in your life today.

If you'd like to further explore and be transformed by these particular attributes of God, we recommend the following books to you.

Sovereignty

Dobson, James. *When God Doesn't Make Sense*. Wheaton, Ill.: Tyndale House Publishers, 1993. Perhaps it is in times of suffering and pain that we are least able to make sense of God's sovereignty. One word, *why*, cries out of the brokenness of our hearts, like a child's wail piercing the night. In this book, Dr. Dobson seeks to shore up and nurture our faith in the God who is "near to the brokenhearted" (Ps. 34:18).

Mercy

Lucado, Max. *He Still Moves Stones*. Dallas, Tex.: Word Publishing, 1993. The Lord's tender and merciful touch emanates from each story Max Lucado tells in this compassionate and hopeful book. Tracing Christ as He met people at their points of pain, Lucado reminds us just how much God cares for the bruised and weary of this world.

Storms, C. Samuel. *To Love Mercy: Becoming a Person of Compassion, Acceptance, and Forgiveness*. Colorado Springs, Colo.: NavPress, 1991. "Blessed are the merciful," Jesus told us, "for they shall receive mercy" (Matt. 5:7). In *To Love Mercy*, author Samuel Storms urges us to avoid hoarding the waters of mercy in our private theological pond. He provides some very practical ideas for channeling God's mercy to others who thirst for it.

Faithfulness

Hurnard, Hannah. *Hinds' Feet on High Places*. Wheaton, Ill.: Tyndale House Publishers, Living Books, 1977. In this classic allegorical story, you'll follow Much-Afraid as she journeys from fear to love, all the while strengthened and guided by her faithful Shepherd.

Holiness

Packer, J. I. *Rediscovering Holiness*. Ann Arbor, Mich.: Servant Publications, Vine Books, 1992. The Lord Himself tells us, "Be holy, for I am holy" (1 Pet. 1:16). J. I. Packer not only helps us learn what holiness is and why it is crucial to our lives, but he shows us how to live a Christlike life of holiness.

Some of these books may be out of print and available only through a library. For those currently available, please contact your local Christian bookstore. Books by Charles R. Swindoll may be obtained through Insight for Living. IFL also offers some books by other authors—please note the ordering information that follows and contact the office that serves you

NOTES

NOTES

NOTES

Notes

NOTES

NOTES

ORDERING INFORMATION

STONES OF REMEMBRANCE
Cassette Tapes and Study Guide

This Bible study guide was designed to be used independently or in conjunction with the broadcast of Chuck Swindoll's taped messages which are listed below. If you would like to order cassette tapes or further copies of this study guide, please see the information given below and the order forms provided at the end of this guide.

		U.S.	Canada
SOR	Study guide	$ 2.95 ea.	$ 3.95 ea.
SORCS	Cassette series, includes all individual tapes, album cover, and one complimentary study guide	16.60	21.75 ea.
SOR 1–2	Individual cassettes, includes messages A and B	6.30 ea.	8.00 ea.

The prices are subject to change without notice.

SOR   1-A: *God's Sovereignty*—Daniel 4:24–37; Job 38, 42; Romans 11:33–36
      B: *God's Mercy*—Selected Scriptures

SOR   2-A: *God's Faithfulness*—Lamentations 3:19–32
      B: *God's Holiness*—Selected Scriptures

How to Order by Phone or FAX
(Credit card orders only)

United States: 1-800-772-8888 from 7:00 A.M. to 4:30 P.M., Pacific time, Monday through Friday
FAX (714) 575-5496 anytime, day or night

Canada: 1-800-663-7639, Vancouver residents call (604) 596-2910 from 7:00 A.M. to 5:00 P.M., Pacific time, Monday through Friday
FAX (604) 596-2975 anytime, day or night

Australia: (03) 872-4606 or FAX (03) 874-8890 from 9:00 A.M. to 5:00 P.M., Monday through Friday

Other International Locations: call the Ordering Services Department in the United States at (714) 575-5000 during the hours listed above.

How to Order by Mail

United States
- Mail to: Ordering Services Department
  Insight for Living
  Post Office Box 69000
  Anaheim, CA 92817-0900
- Sales tax: California residents add 7.25%.
- Shipping: add 10% of the total order amount for first-class delivery. (Otherwise, allow four to six weeks for fourth-class delivery.)
- Payment: personal checks, money orders, credit cards (Visa, Master-Card, Discover Card, and American Express). No invoices or COD orders available.
- $10 fee for *any* returned check.

Canada
- Mail to: Insight for Living Ministries
  Post Office Box 2510
  Vancouver, BC V6B 3W7
- Sales tax: please add 7% GST. British Columbia residents also add 7% sales tax (on tapes or cassette series).
- Shipping: included in prices listed above.
- Payment: personal checks, money orders, credit cards (Visa, Master-Card). No invoices or COD orders available.
- Delivery: approximately four weeks.

Australia, New Zealand, or Papua New Guinea
- Mail to: Insight for Living, Inc.
  GPO Box 2823 EE
  Melbourne, Victoria 3001, Australia
- Shipping and delivery time: please see chart that follows.
- Payment: personal checks payable in U.S. funds, international money orders, or credit cards (Visa, MasterCard).

Other International Locations
- Mail to: Ordering Services Department
  Insight for Living
  Post Office Box 69000
  Anaheim, CA 92817-0900

- Shipping and delivery time: please see chart that follows.
- Payment: personal checks payable in U.S. funds, international money orders, or credit cards (Visa, MasterCard, and American Express).

Type of Shipping	Postage Cost	Delivery
Surface	10% of total order*	6 to 10 weeks
Airmail	25% of total order*	under 6 weeks

*Use U.S. price as a base.

Our Guarantee

Your complete satisfaction is our top priority here at Insight for Living. If you're not completely satisfied with anything you order, please return it for full credit, a refund, or a replacement, as *you* prefer.

Insight for Living Catalog

The Insight for Living catalog features study guides, tapes, and books by a variety of Christian authors. To obtain a free copy, call us at the numbers listed above.

Order Form
United States, Australia, and Other International Locations
(Canadian residents please use order form on reverse side.)

SORCS represents the entire *Stones of Remembrance* series in a special album cover, while SOR 1–2 are the individual tapes included in the series. SOR represents this study guide, should you desire to order additional copies.

SOR	Study guide	$ 2.95 ea.
SORCS	Cassette series, includes all individual tapes, album cover, and one complimentary study guide	16.60
SOR 1–2	Individual cassettes, includes messages A and B	6.30 ea.

Product Code	Product Description	Quantity	Unit Price	Total
			$	$
		Subtotal		
	California Residents—Sales Tax *Add 7.25% of subtotal.*			
	U.S. First-Class Shipping *For faster delivery, add 10% for postage and handling.*			
	Non-United States Residents *U.S. price plus 10% surface postage or 25% airmail.*			
	Gift to Insight for Living *Tax-deductible in the United States.*			
	Total Amount Due *Please do not send cash.*		$	

Prices are subject to change without notice.

Payment by: ❏ Check or money order payable to Insight for Living ❏ Credit card

(Circle one):   Visa   MasterCard   Discover Card   American Express

Number _____

Expiration Date _____   Signature _____
We cannot process your credit card purchase without your signature.

Name _____

Address _____

City _____   State _____

Zip Code _____   Country _____

Telephone (___) _____   Radio Station ___ ___ ___ ___
If questions arise concerning your order, we may need to contact you.

Mail this order form to the Ordering Services Department at one of these addresses:

Insight for Living
Post Office Box 69000, Anaheim, CA 92817-0900

Insight for Living, Inc.
GPO Box 2823 EE, Melbourne, VIC 3001, Australia

ECFA
MEMBER

Order Form
Canadian Residents

(Residents of the United States, Australia, and other international locations,
please use order form on reverse side.)

SORCS represents the entire *Stones of Remembrance* series in a special album cover, while
SOR 1–2 are the individual tapes included in the series. SOR represents this study guide,
should you desire to order additional copies.

SOR	Study guide	$ 3.95 ea.
SORCS	Cassette series,	21.75
	includes all individual tapes, album cover,	
	and one complimentary study guide	
SOR 1–2	Individual cassettes,	8.00 ea.
	includes messages A and B	

Product Code	Product Description	Quantity	Unit Price	Total
			$	$
		Subtotal		
		Add 7% GST		
		British Columbia Residents *Add 7% sales tax on individual tapes or cassette series.*		
		Gift to Insight for Living Ministries *Tax-deductible in Canada.*		
		Total Amount Due *Please do not send cash.*	$	

Prices are subject to change without notice.

Payment by: ❑ Check or money order payable to Insight for Living Ministries
❑ Credit card

(Circle one): Visa   MasterCard   Number _____

Expiration Date _____   Signature _____
We cannot process your credit card purchase without your signature.

Name _____

Address _____

City _____   Province _____

Postal Code _____   Country _____

Telephone (__) _____   Radio Station ____ ____ ____ ____
If questions arise concerning your order, we may need to contact you.

Mail this order form to the Ordering Services Department at the following address:

Insight for Living Ministries
Post Office Box 2510
Vancouver, BC, Canada V6B 3W7

Order Form
United States, Australia, and Other International Locations
(Canadian residents please use order form on reverse side.)

SORCS represents the entire *Stones of Remembrance* series in a special album cover, while SOR 1–2 are the individual tapes included in the series. SOR represents this study guide, should you desire to order additional copies.

SOR	Study guide	$ 2.95 ea.
SORCS	Cassette series, includes all individual tapes, album cover, and one complimentary study guide	16.60
SOR 1–2	Individual cassettes, includes messages A and B	6.30 ea.

Product Code	Product Description	Quantity	Unit Price	Total
			$	$
		Subtotal		
	California Residents—Sales Tax *Add 7.25% of subtotal.*			
	U.S. First-Class Shipping *For faster delivery, add 10% for postage and handling.*			
	Non-United States Residents *U.S. price plus 10% surface postage or 25% airmail.*			
	Gift to Insight for Living *Tax-deductible in the United States.*			
	Total Amount Due *Please do not send cash.*		$	

Prices are subject to change without notice.

Payment by: ❏ Check or money order payable to Insight for Living ❏ Credit card

(Circle one):   Visa   MasterCard   Discover Card   American Express

Number _____

Expiration Date _____   Signature _____
We cannot process your credit card purchase without your signature.

Name _____

Address _____

City _____   State _____

Zip Code _____   Country _____

Telephone (____) _____   Radio Station ____ ____ ____ ____
If questions arise concerning your order, we may need to contact you.

Mail this order form to the Ordering Services Department at one of these addresses:

Insight for Living
Post Office Box 69000, Anaheim, CA 92817-0900

Insight for Living, Inc.
GPO Box 2823 EE, Melbourne, VIC 3001, Australia

ECFA MEMBER

Order Form
Canadian Residents
(Residents of the United States, Australia, and other international locations, please use order form on reverse side.)

SORCS represents the entire *Stones of Remembrance* series in a special album cover, while SOR 1–2 are the individual tapes included in the series. SOR represents this study guide, should you desire to order additional copies.

SOR	Study guide	$ 3.95 ea.
SORCS	Cassette series,	21.75
	includes all individual tapes, album cover,	
	and one complimentary study guide	
SOR 1–2	Individual cassettes,	8.00 ea.
	includes messages A and B	

Product Code	Product Description	Quantity	Unit Price	Total
			$	$
		Subtotal		
		Add 7% GST		
		British Columbia Residents *Add 7% sales tax on individual tapes or cassette series.*		
		Gift to Insight for Living Ministries *Tax-deductible in Canada.*		
		Total Amount Due *Please do not send cash.*	$	

Prices are subject to change without notice.

Payment by: ❑ Check or money order payable to Insight for Living Ministries
❑ Credit card

(Circle one): Visa MasterCard Number _____

Expiration Date _____ Signature _____
We cannot process your credit card purchase without your signature.

Name _____

Address _____

City _____ Province _____

Postal Code _____ Country _____

Telephone ( ) _____ Radio Station ____ ____ ____ ____
If questions arise concerning your order, we may need to contact you.

Mail this order form to the Ordering Services Department at the following address:

Insight for Living Ministries
Post Office Box 2510
Vancouver, BC, Canada V6B 3W7

Order Form
United States, Australia, and Other International Locations
(Canadian residents please use order form on reverse side.)

SORCS represents the entire *Stones of Remembrance* series in a special album cover, while SOR 1–2 are the individual tapes included in the series. SOR represents this study guide, should you desire to order additional copies.

SOR	Study guide	$ 2.95 ea.
SORCS	Cassette series,	16.60
	includes all individual tapes, album cover, and one complimentary study guide	
SOR 1–2	Individual cassettes,	6.30 ea.
	includes messages A and B	

Product Code	Product Description	Quantity	Unit Price	Total
			$	$
		Subtotal		
	California Residents—Sales Tax *Add 7.25% of subtotal.*			
	U.S. First-Class Shipping *For faster delivery, add 10% for postage and handling.*			
	Non-United States Residents *U.S. price plus 10% surface postage or 25% airmail.*			
	Gift to Insight for Living *Tax-deductible in the United States.*			
	Total Amount Due *Please do not send cash.*		$	

Prices are subject to change without notice.

Payment by: ❑ Check or money order payable to Insight for Living   ❑ Credit card

(Circle one):   Visa   MasterCard   Discover Card   American Express

Number _____

Expiration Date _____   Signature _____
We cannot process your credit card purchase without your signature.

Name _____

Address _____

City _____   State _____

Zip Code _____   Country _____

Telephone (___) _____   Radio Station ____ ____ ____ ____
If questions arise concerning your order, we may need to contact you.

Mail this order form to the Ordering Services Department at one of these addresses:

Insight for Living
Post Office Box 69000, Anaheim, CA 92817-0900

Insight for Living, Inc.
GPO Box 2823 EE, Melbourne, VIC 3001, Australia

ECFA MEMBER

Order Form
Canadian Residents
(Residents of the United States, Australia, and other international locations,
please use order form on reverse side.)

SORCS represents the entire *Stones of Remembrance* series in a special album cover, while
SOR 1–2 are the individual tapes included in the series. SOR represents this study guide,
should you desire to order additional copies.

SOR	**Study guide**	**$ 3.95 ea.**
SORCS	**Cassette series,**	**21.75**
	includes all individual tapes, album cover,	
	and one complimentary study guide	
SOR 1–2	**Individual cassettes,**	**8.00 ea.**
	includes messages A and B	

Product Code	Product Description	Quantity	Unit Price	Total
			$	$
		Subtotal		
		Add 7% GST		
	British Columbia Residents *Add 7% sales tax on individual tapes or cassette series.*			
	Gift to Insight for Living Ministries *Tax-deductible in Canada.*			
	Total Amount Due *Please do not send cash.*		$	

Prices are subject to change without notice.

Payment by: ❏ Check or money order payable to Insight for Living Ministries
❏ Credit card

(Circle one): Visa   MasterCard   Number _____

Expiration Date _____   Signature _____
We cannot process your credit card purchase without your signature.

Name _____

Address _____

City _____   Province _____

Postal Code _____   Country _____

Telephone (__) _____   Radio Station ___ ___ ___ ___
If questions arise concerning your order, we may need to contact you.

Mail this order form to the Ordering Services Department at the following address:

Insight for Living Ministries
Post Office Box 2510
Vancouver, BC, Canada V6B 3W7